"One thing is clear to me: We, as human beings, must be willing to accept people who are different from ourselves."

— BARBARA JORDAN

BARBARA JORDAN
AFRICAN AMERICAN POLITICIAN

By Joseph D. McNair

The Child's World

GRAPHIC DESIGN
Robert E. Bonaker / Graphic Design & Consulting Co.

PROJECT COORDINATOR
James R. Rothaus / James R. Rothaus & Associates

EDITORIAL DIRECTION
Elizabeth Sirimarco Budd

COVER PHOTO
Portrait of Barbara Jordan
©Bettmann/CORBIS

Library of Congress Cataloging-in-Publication Data
McNair, Joseph D.
Barbara Jordan: African American Politician / by Joseph D. McNair.
p. cm.
Includes index.
Summary: Traces the life and work of this African-American
woman who was a respected politician, teacher, and
spokeswoman for democracy.
ISBN 1-56766-741-4 (lib. bdg. : acid-free paper)

1. Jordan, Barbara, 1936– — Juvenile literature. 2. Legislators —
United States — Biography — Juvenile literature. 3. Afro-American
women legislators — Biography — Juvenile literature. 4. United
States. Congress. House — Biography — Juvenile literature. 5. Afro-
American women legislators — Texas — Biography — Juvenile
literature. 6. Texas — Politics and government — 1951 — Juvenile
literature. [1. Jordan, Barbara, 1936– 2. Legislators. 3. Afro-
Americans — Biography. 4. Women — Biography.] I. Title

E840.8.J62 M38 2000
328.73'092 — dc21   00-026854
[B]

Contents

Political Pioneer

Mwalimu the storyteller was pleased. It was another Thursday evening, and the church basement was full of interested young people.

"Tonight, children, I will tell you a story of an African American woman who stood up to defend the U.S. Constitution — a black woman who stood up to the most powerful man in the world."

You could hear a pin drop. Mwalimu sat in a simple folding chair with his carved ebony cane across his lap. He was dressed in a flowing white Nigerian *baban riga* (big gown) and wore an embroidered *huna* (cap) of white and gold. Nearly 300 pounds, he sat on that folding chair as if it were a throne.

"Washington, D.C., is the capital city of this great nation, children. It is a place of power. They tell me that the man who designed this city wanted it to represent freedom.

"But children, I'm here to tell you that freedom is not free! The freedoms we enjoy today were fought for and dearly won. And if we don't hold on to them like life itself, they will slip away.

"No one knows this better than the children of Africa — you, our parents, our parents' parents, and me," he said gently, like thunder rumbling in the distance.

"But let me get on with my story. On the evening of July 25, 1974, Americans of every kind sat in front of their television sets. The president of the United States, Richard Nixon, was in deep trouble, children. The government had accused him of terrible crimes — crimes against the Constitution. If found guilty, he could be removed from office.

"A **committee** from the U.S. Congress was looking at the **evidence** against our country's president. The American people wanted to know if there was enough evidence to **impeach** him.

©Bettmann/CORBIS

As a member of the House of Representatives, Barbara Jordan (front row, second from left) was part of a special committee that had to decide whether to impeach President Richard Nixon. It was only the second time in U.S. history that Congress had been called upon to make such an important decision.

JUST AFTER RICHARD NIXON RESIGNED AS
PRESIDENT OF THE UNITED STATES, HE
BOARDED A HELICOPTER ON THE WHITE
HOUSE LAWN THAT WOULD TAKE HIM TO
HIS HOME STATE OF CALIFORNIA.

"Now, children, it is a serious thing to impeach the president of the United States. To impeach someone means accusing a leader of doing something wrong. Impeach the president of the United States? Well, that means to accuse the president of serious crimes against the Constitution — and against the country. If the U.S. Senate finds the president guilty, he will be removed from office.

"At 8:30 that evening in 1974, the television cameras began to roll. People around the nation tuned in to hear the committee's final words.

"The first to speak was a large, round-faced, black woman. She was a congresswoman from Texas. Her voice was magical — deep, rich, and musical. It grabbed people's attention and held it.

"The preamble of the Constitution, children, begins with the phrase, 'We the people of the United States.' The congresswoman told America that when the Constitution was written in 1787, African people in America were not considered part of 'the people.'

" 'I have finally been included in We the People,' she said on national television. 'My faith in the Constitution is whole, it is complete, it is total.' Barbara Jordan said she would not stand by and watch as the nation's president ignored the Constitution.

"For 11 minutes, children, she taught the nation. She explained the evidence against President Nixon. She explained that he had used his power to hurt people. She told Americans how government workers had helped hide his crimes. She said that he had lied to the nation.

"Over the next two days, 37 members of Congress spoke to the nation. Many were impressive, and many spoke well. But no one captured the country's attention like the African American congresswoman from Texas.

"Fifteen days later, on August 9, 1974, President Richard M. Nixon resigned.

"Who was this African woman, this black congresswoman from Texas? Now I'd like to tell you her story," said Mwalimu, knowing that he had the children's attention.

The Jordan Family

Barbara Charline Jordan was born on February 21, 1936. When her father saw her, his first comment was, "Why is she so dark?" Skin color meant a great deal to Ben Jordan. In those days, African Americans with the lightest skin often were treated better than those who had darker skin.

Fortunately for Barbara, if she wasn't the "apple of her father's eye," she was her Grandpa Patten's favorite. Grandpa Patten was her mother's father. He knew that there was more to life than having light skin. He told Barbara that she was beautiful. He took care of her on Sundays when she was too young to go to church with the rest of the family. Barbara was proud of her Grandpa. He was a brave man who wasn't afraid of anything.

When Barbara started grade school, she was a "cut up." She talked out of turn, told jokes, passed notes, and played jokes on her friends. She often got into trouble. If Barbara came home with bad grades, her mother punished her with a spanking. Her Daddy never spanked her. But his few scolding words hurt more than all her mother's spankings put together.

The last person Barbara wanted was to disappoint her father. She started going to church with her family at the Good Hope Baptist Church. She stopped acting out at school and became an excellent student. Her grades had always been good, but they got even better. With pride, she came home with an "A" in five classes and a "B" in one class. She showed the report card to her father.

His comment was, "Why did you get a 'B'? You can't get anywhere with a 'B'!" Barbara made up her mind to get an "A" in every class from that day on.

Courtesy of the Barbara Jordan Archives, Texas Southern University

BARBARA'S GRANDPA PATTEN RECOGNIZED THAT BARBARA WAS A SPECIAL PERSON. HE TREATED HER WITH RESPECT AND AFFECTION.

Courtesy of the Barbara Jordan Archives, Texas Southern University

BARBARA (CENTER) IS SHOWN IN THIS FAMILY PHOTOGRAPH WITH HER TWO OLDER SISTERS.

When Barbara started high school, she wanted to be popular. She had a big problem, though. She didn't look like the popular girls at school. They were all light-skinned, and she was dark. They were slim and pretty. She was tall and weighed 175 pounds.

She had another problem, too — her father! Ben Jordan had become a **pastor** at a Baptist church. Now he was stricter than ever. He had more rules about where she could go and whom she could see.

Even with these strikes against her, Barbara was determined to be popular. She learned to smile a lot. She changed her hairstyle. She began to wear jewelry and dress like the popular girls. She went to the football games.

Barbara and her older sister Bennie were part of a singing group. Barbara had a nice, deep singing voice, but her speaking voice was even better. When the group was invited to perform at churches, Barbara would recite religious poetry. She soon realized that she could get the audience's attention with her speaking voice. She discovered that she could make people feel good or even make them cry when she recited poems and stories. She felt good about herself when she spoke in front of people.

Barbara started speaking at school events. She was amazed at how easy it was to get other students to listen to her. Even if she didn't look like the popular crowd, she still had a chance to succeed at school. She could be the most **outstanding** student. For the next three years, that became her goal.

One of Barbara's teachers heard Barbara speak at a student meeting. He invited her to join the **debate team.** By her senior year, she was the team star. She was also a member of all of the important school clubs. Every teacher knew her by name. Most important of all, Barbara had discovered what she was going to do with her life. In 1951, Barbara came face-to-face with a vision of her future when she heard Edith Spurlock Sampson speak.

BARBARA CAME FROM A PART OF HOUSTON CALLED THE FIFTH WARD, SHOWN IN THIS PHOTOGRAPH. MOST OF THE PEOPLE WHO LIVED THERE WERE AFRICAN AMERICAN.

Sampson was an African American lawyer who had achieved great things. She came to Barbara's school to speak to the students. Sampson encouraged young African Americans to go to college and to study law. Barbara had never seen a woman — especially a black woman — who was so successful and confident.

Sampson made a career in law seem like the best thing a young black woman could do with her life. When she finished speaking to the students, Barbara knew she was going to study law. That year, the state of Texas had less than 20 African American lawyers. That did not stop Barbara from aiming high.

At Phillis Wheatley High School, Barbara was selected as "Girl of the Year" in honor of her achievements. All of the teachers voted for her. Barbara's father was so proud that he cried. At last, he approved of his youngest daughter.

BARBARA DID NOT ALWAYS FEEL POPULAR WHEN SHE WAS IN HIGH SCHOOL. SOME OF THE OTHER GIRLS WERE PRETTIER THAN SHE WAS, BUT SHE WAS DETERMINED TO STAND OUT IN ANOTHER WAY. SHE BECAME THE VERY BEST STUDENT SHE COULD. SHE SOON DECIDED SHE WANTED TO GO TO COLLEGE AND BECOME A LAWYER.

Separate but Equal?

In 1896, many years before Barbara Jordan was born, the United States Supreme Court made an important decision. It decided that keeping black people and white people separate was legal. African Americans could have schools and churches, but they were separate from white schools and churches. People called the court's decision the "separate but equal" rule.

The country began creating "separate but equal" schools, neighborhoods, theaters, restaurants, and parks. People posted signs that read "For Whites Only" or "Colored Only." Public places in much of the country, especially in the South, were now legally **segregated.** "Separate but equal" became the rule of the land, and that included the state of Texas.

In 1947, a college for African Americans opened in Texas. White people did not want blacks attending their colleges, so they created the Texas State University for Negroes. In September of 1952, Barbara Jordan started school there. By that time, the school had been renamed Texas Southern University (TSU).

The first thing Barbara did at TSU was run for class president. She lost the election. It looked as if life at college would be much as it had been in high school. It was her classmates with the lightest skin and eyes, with the smoothest hair and the slimmest bodies, who would win the popularity contests. Barbara knew she would succeed only by being the very best student she could be.

DURING HER SECOND YEAR, BARBARA (FRONT ROW, RIGHT SIDE)
JOINED THE TSU DEBATE TEAM. DEBATING WAS SOMETHING
SHE DID WELL, AND IT MADE HER FEEL GOOD ABOUT HERSELF.

Just as she did in high school, Barbara decided to be the school's most outstanding student. She joined the debate team, and it became an important part of her college life. The team traveled all over the country and won most of its contests.

During her second year of college, the TSU debate team became the first African American team to be invited to a well-known tournament at Baylor University. It was the first time Barbara competed against white students. She won first place in one part of the tournament. Winning that contest made her believe that she could win every time.

During her senior year, Barbara was not only a champion debater, she also was editor of the yearbook, a member of the student council, and a leader at her **sorority.** If she was not the most popular student at TSU, she was certainly the best known.

In 1956, Barbara enrolled in Boston University to study law. It was one of only two American colleges that had always admitted black students. For years, the college had accepted bright African American students from all over the country. Barbara's father knew the school was expensive, but he promised to help her in whatever way he could. "If you want to go, we'll manage," he told her.

Barbara was lonely and afraid in Boston. She had never been so far from home for such a long period of time. She had been the top student at TSU. But that school was very different from Boston University. Now she had to study longer and harder than her fellow students just to keep up. Sometimes, she wanted to quit and go home.

In her darkest hour, she prayed for help. Reverend Howard Thurman helped to answer her prayers. Dr. Thurman was a professor of **theology.** He also led religious services at the school's chapel. Dr. Thurman encouraged Barbara. She met with him as often as his busy schedule allowed.

Junior Class Officers

OTIS KING .... *President*
BARBARA JORDAN .... *Vice President*
MILDRED POWELL .... *Secretary*
DELORES TARVER .... *Treasurer*

THIS PAGE FROM BARBARA'S COLLEGE YEARBOOK SHOWS HER (SECOND FROM LEFT) WITH THE OTHER JUNIOR CLASS OFFICERS. OTHER STUDENTS VOTED FOR THEM TO BE THE LEADERS OF THEIR CLASS.

BARBARA AND OTHER MEMBERS OF HER DEBATE TEAM ARE SHOWN HERE ADMIRING SOME OF THE TROPHIES THEY WON. BARBARA'S SKILL AS A DEBATER PREPARED HER TO BECOME A LAWYER. SHE KNEW THAT LAWYERS NEED EXCELLENT SPEAKING SKILLS.

A quiet and gentle black man, many people thought Thurman was one of the greatest **preachers** in the country. Barbara loved listening to him speak at the chapel. She liked his **sermons** so much that she tried hard to remember his words. Then she would recite them to her roommates.

Something terrible happened during Barbara's last months at Boston University. Her beloved grandfather, the man who first told her that she was someone special, was hit by a freight train. Ed Patten lived long enough after the accident for Barbara to get to Houston so she could say good-bye. Dr. Thurman helped her get through this tragedy.

After Barbara graduated, she thought about staying in Boston. But she decided to move back to Houston. In October of 1959, she passed the state exam that allowed her to **practice** law in Texas. She became the third African American woman to practice law in Texas.

Courtesy of the Barbara Jordan Archives, Texas Southern University

ONE ACTIVITY BARBARA ENJOYED AT TSU WAS HER ROLE AS THE YEARBOOK EDITOR. IN COLLEGE, SHE FOUND TIME TO TAKE PART IN MANY ACTIVITIES AND STILL MAKE GOOD GRADES. BUT SHE WASN'T PREPARED FOR HOW DIFFICULT LAW SCHOOL WOULD BE. SHE HAD TO SPEND MOST OF HER TIME STUDYING. ALL BARBARA'S HARD WORK PAID OFF WHEN SHE BECAME A LAWYER IN 1959.

The Politician

"**S**ome people say, children, that each of us is born to do something special!"

Mwalimu was enjoying himself now. He stood up and began to pace in front of his audience, tapping his cane as he walked.

"And they say that we can spend our whole lives trying to figure out what that special something is. At 23 years old, living again at her father's house, Barbara Charline Jordan was trying to be a lawyer. She might have been pretty good at it, but her heart just wasn't in it. She began to dream of a career in **politics.**

"Barbara Charline found herself volunteering to help get the black community to vote in the 1960 election. She did anything she could to get the word out to black voters. One day, a speaker at a rally didn't show up. The rally organizers needed an African American to speak. They asked Barbara, knowing what a good speaker she was.

"The magic was there from the moment she opened her mouth. Suddenly, she found a use for her special talents. She saw hopeful African Americans looking to her for leadership. She knew what she had to do. Barbara was going to become a **politician.**"

Mwalimu looked out at the children for a moment, and then continued his story.

"By 1962, it seemed as if Barbara might have a chance to win a seat in the Texas Senate, the group of elected leaders who make laws for the state. She decided to run for office. But even if Barbara got the vote of every African American in Houston, she couldn't win.

Courtesy Texas Senate Media Service

BARBARA WORKED AS A LAWYER IN HOUSTON FOR A FEW YEARS, BUT SHE SOON
REALIZED THAT SHE HAD ANOTHER DREAM. SHE WANTED A CAREER IN POLITICS.
AS A POLITICIAN, SHE FELT SURE SHE COULD MAKE A DIFFERENCE.

Houston was still segregated, and **prejudice** was a problem. Barbara couldn't win because very few white people would vote for a black **candidate.** Barbara lost the 1962 and 1964 elections — even though she won most of the black community's vote. Finally, in the 1966 election, she won a seat in the Texas State Senate.

On January 10, 1967, Barbara Jordan was sworn in as the first female African American senator in Texas history.

The Texas Senate had always been made up of white men. They had little contact with black women. In fact, most of the senators believed that black women were supposed to be maids and nannies, not politicians. People who supported Barbara wondered if these men would cooperate with her.

Barbara was determined to succeed. She quickly learned how the Senate worked. She learned how to get other senators to pass the **bills** she supported. She got to know the most powerful senators. She cooperated with them, even when she knew most of these men thought she had no business being in the Senate.

Barbara made the other senators forget that she was a black woman. As she worked with them, she learned from them. The Senate leaders soon saw how **capable** she was. By the end of her first **term,** many people thought Barbara was the most skillful member of the Texas Senate.

In 1969, during her second term, Barbara was responsible for a major change in Texas: a new **minimum wage** law. A U.S. law said that no worker could be paid less than $1.60 an hour. But Texas never accepted this law. Most Texas employers did not want a minimum wage. If they could pay workers less, the employers made more money. Most of the Texas senators were against a minimum wage law, too — but not Barbara Jordan.

25

Courtesy of the Barbara Jordan Archives, Texas Southern University

BARBARA'S SKILL WON THE ADMIRATION OF A
VERY IMPORTANT TEXAN: PRESIDENT LYNDON
B. JOHNSON. HE MADE IT A POINT TO ASK
BARBARA FOR HER OPINIONS. HE BELIEVED
THAT INTELLIGENT POLITICIANS LIKE HER
COULD ACCOMPLISH A GREAT DEAL.

With Barbara's effort, the state passed a law making it illegal to pay a worker less than $1.25 per hour. Barbara still thought this was too little, but she was pleased that the law had passed at all, since so few senators supported it.

Barbara had another important bill passed in her second term. It helped workers who were hurt on the job. By law, if someone was injured at work, employers had to pay the person's medical costs. They also had to pay a portion of the worker's wages. Texas paid injured workers less than almost any other state in the country. Barbara's hard work helped win an increase in the money paid to these workers.

Barbara played a role in many other important laws during her time with the Texas Senate. One gave teachers a pay raise. Another created public kindergartens. A third provided money to companies that hired physically challenged workers. She even succeeded in getting the Senate to end many state segregation laws. Barbara became known as someone who would help those who most needed the government's support.

Barbara's hard work earned the attention of the most important Texan in the country — Lyndon Baines Johnson, the 36th president of the United States. He liked what she had to say, and he liked the way she said it. After all, she was a Texan, and Johnson was proud of all good things from Texas. President Johnson told other Texas politicians that Barbara Jordan was one of his friends.

In 1971, Houston's mayor, Louis Welch, declared that October 1 was "Barbara Jordan Appreciation Day." Lyndon Johnson was the special guest at a dinner held to celebrate the day. In a speech before the gathering, the former president said, "Barbara Jordan proved to us that black was beautiful before we knew what it meant. Wherever she goes, she is going to be at the top. Wherever Barbara goes, all of us are going to be behind her."

Congresswoman Jordan

In 1972, Barbara decided to run for a seat in the U.S. Congress. She spent much of her time that year **campaigning** to win the election. If she did win, she would be leaving the Texas Senate and moving to the nation's capital city.

Texas had a tradition: One day each year, the governor left town. On that day, a leader from the Texas Senate became the honorary governor for the day. On June 10, 1972, it was Barbara Jordan who was named as governor. Such an honor would have been impossible for any other black person in Texas. At the ceremony held at the Senate chamber, black Texans filled the room.

Barbara Jordan called the celebration a "black day" for Texas. "Who would have thought," Barbara said at the ceremony, "that a product of Phillis Wheatley High School and Texas Southern University could become governor of Texas, even for a day?"

One African American at the event was especially important. Barbara's father, Ben Jordan, was there to see his daughter receive the honor. Although very sick, he was determined to be there. When the audience stood to applaud, Ben Jordan had to be helped to his feet. When Barbara accepted the honor, her father cried.

Unfortunately, Ben Jordan collapsed right after the ceremony. An ambulance took him to the hospital. One day later, Ben Jordan died. His dying words were: "I wanted to see this day ...." Throughout his daughter's life, Ben Jordan had pushed her and challenged her. Sometimes he made her angry. She had always wanted to show him that she was someone special. But Ben Jordan had also supported Barbara in everything she did. She was greatly saddened by his death.

Courtesy of the Barbara Jordan Archives, Texas Southern University

ON JUNE 10, 1972, BARBARA JORDAN RECEIVED THE SPECIAL HONOR OF
BEING THE GOVERNOR OF TEXAS FOR A DAY. HER PARENTS WERE AT THE
CEREMONY TO SHOW HOW PROUD OF HER THEY WERE. HERE THEY ARE
SEATED TO THE LEFT OF BARBARA AS SHE TAKES THE OATH OF OFFICE.

Later that year, on November 12, Barbara Jordan won her election to the U.S. Congress. She received a huge number of votes. The following January, she was sworn in as a member of the U.S. Congress. She was re-elected twice, serving a total of six years.

Shortly after becoming a U.S. congresswoman, Barbara learned that she had a serious disease called **multiple sclerosis.** Even though she was ill, she served her country with great skill. She tried to keep the illness a secret, too. Barbara did not want people to worry about her.

Three events during her time in Congress mark the high points of Barbara's political career. The first was her role in the impeachment of President Nixon. Messages flooded into her office after her famous speech on television. The American people let Barbara know that they had heard her. They let her know that she gave them hope in the government once more.

Barbara also helped pass the 1975 Voting Rights Act. Ever since African Americans were first allowed to vote, some white people in the South had tried to stop them from doing so. In 1965, Congress passed an act that made it easier for African Americans to vote. With this new law, the government made sure that no one stopped blacks and other minorities from voting.

The 1965 law was supposed to end on August 7, 1975. President Ford did not want to renew it. Powerful members of Congress were also against it. But Barbara Jordan's efforts encouraged the House of Representatives to pass the bill on June 3.

BARBARA BELIEVED THAT SHE COULD HELP AFRICAN AMERICANS THE MOST BY COOPERATING WITH OTHER MEMBERS OF CONGRESS, NOT BY TRYING TO BRING ABOUT BIG CHANGES ALL AT ONCE. SHE ALSO WANTED TO REPRESENT EVERYONE WHO HAD VOTED FOR HER, NOT JUST AFRICAN AMERICANS. SHE ONCE SAID, "I AM NEITHER A BLACK POLITICIAN NOR A FEMALE POLITICIAN, JUST A POLITICIAN."

Perhaps the most important event in Barbara Jordan's career was her speech at the 1976 Democratic National **Convention**. At this event, the Democratic **political party** chose its candidate for the next election. Barbara was one of the two most important speakers at the week-long convention. Senator John Glenn, astronaut and American hero, was the other. On that July evening in New York City, Glenn spoke first. Unfortunately, the audience wasn't paying much attention to his speech.

When Barbara stepped onto the stage, the crowd began to applaud — even before she started speaking. People remembered her and her role in the Nixon resignation. When she started to speak, there was a hush throughout the convention hall:

"It was 144 years ago that members of the Democratic Party first met," said Barbara, "to select their presidential candidate. Since that time, Democrats continued to **convene** once every four years to draft a party **platform** and nominate a presidential candidate. Our meeting this week is a continuation of that tradition.

But there is something different. There is something special about tonight. What is different? What is special? I, Barbara Jordan, am keynote speaker."

Every Democrat in the house was on their feet cheering. Some were even crying. Barbara Jordan was the first black American to ever speak at the Democratic National Convention. Barbara spoke for 20 minutes. Her speech was interrupted 20 times by thunderous applause. It was her finest hour as an African American, as a woman, and as a citizen of the United States. Her musical voice reached out to Americans everywhere and touched their hearts. Some people even wondered why she wasn't the one running for president!

Democrat Jimmy Carter was elected the 39th president of the United States in November of 1976. Two years later, Barbara decided not to run for Congress again. Unfortunately, she was becoming very ill.

©Owen Franken/CORBIS

BARBARA JORDAN RECEIVED A STANDING OVATION BEFORE SHE EVEN BEGAN SPEAKING AT THE DEMOCRATIC NATIONAL CONVENTION IN 1976.

The Spirit Remains

"The ways of the Creator are mysterious indeed, children."

Mwalimu said this with a sigh as he sat back down in his chair. He seemed exhausted. His voice was no more than a low rumble now.

"Barbara Charline Jordan was a black girl from Texas. People thought she was too fat, too black, and too ugly to amount to anything. This same girl taught America what it meant to be an American. She found America's heart, and she spoke to it. She helped America see the very best of her.

"In early 1979, Barbara retired from politics. Around that time, someone asked her what she felt was the biggest accomplishment of her career. Barbara replied that she was most proud of giving a voice to people who had never before had a say in their own government.

"Barbara may have left Congress, but she kept busy. She taught law at the University of Texas until her death in 1996. Cancer and multiple sclerosis brought her brilliant life to a close.

"On January 17, 1996, the day after Martin Luther King, Jr.'s, birthday, Barbara left this world. Four days later, friends and fans gathered to say good-bye at the Good Hope Baptist Church in Houston. Even President Bill Clinton was there.

"I believe, children, that Barbara Jordan is talking to America still. Her spirit is there in the shadows of the Capitol, where bills are written and important decisions are made. Her spirit is in all laws that help people, which strive for the freedom and equality promised by the Constitution.

"I leave you with this, children. Barbara is the spirit of all that is good about American politics." And with that, Mwalimu's story was finished.

Reuters/Ray Stubblebine/Archive Photos

BARBARA SMILED AS SHE LISTENED TO THE CHEERS OF PEOPLE AT THE 1992 DEMOCRATIC CONVENTION. BARBARA WAS NO LONGER A MEMBER OF CONGRESS, BUT SHE STILL INSPIRED OTHER POLITICIANS WITH HER WORDS.

Timeline

1936 Barbara Jordan is born on February 21 in Houston, Texas.

1948 Barbara enters Phillis Wheatley High School.

1952 After graduating from high school, Barbara enters Texas Southern University (TSU). She focuses her studies on political science and history.

1956 Barbara graduates from TSU and enters Boston University Law School.

1959 Barbara earns her law degree. In October, she receives her license to practice law in Texas.

1960 Barbara opens a law office in Houston. In her spare time, she works to encourage African Americans to vote.

1966 Barbara runs for the Texas Senate. She is elected and becomes the first black member of the state's Senate since 1883. She is also the first African American female elected to the Texas Senate.

1967 Barbara is sworn in as a member of the Texas Senate on January 10.

1969 Barbara begins her second term with the Texas Senate.

1971 Houston's mayor names October 1 "Barbara Jordan Appreciation Day." Lyndon Johnson, the former U.S. president, is the special guest at a dinner in her honor and gives a speech praising Barbara.

1972 Barbara is named "Governor for a Day."

1972 Barbara decides to run for the United States Congress. She wins the election in November.

1973 Barbara is sworn in as a member of the United States House of Representatives.

1974 Barbara is a member of a special congressional committee that leads President Nixon's impeachment hearings. Her speech is nationally televised on July 25.

1976 Barbara gives the keynote speech at the Democratic National Convention.

1979 Barbara takes a position teaching law at the University of Texas.

1992 Barbara is asked to speak again at the Democratic National Convention.

1996 Barbara Jordan dies on January 17.

Glossary

bills (BILZ)
Bills are ideas for new laws that are presented to a group of lawmakers. Senator Jordan learned how to get bills passed.

campaigning (kam-PAYN)
When candidates campaign, they do things (such as giving speeches and meeting voters) to help them win an election. Barbara Jordan spent 1972 campaigning to win an election.

candidate (KAN-dih-dayt)
A candidate is a person who is running for a public office. Barbara Jordan was a candidate for the U.S. House of Representatives in the 1972 election.

capable (KAY-puh-bul)
If someone is capable, he or she is skillful or able to do something well. Barbara Jordan was capable of doing many things.

committee (kuh-MIH-tee)
A committee is a group of people chosen to do something important. Barbara Jordan was part of the committee in Congress that looked at evidence against President Nixon.

convene (kun-VEEN)
If people convene, they gather at a meeting to discuss something. Members of the Democratic Party convene to choose a presidential candidate.

convention (kun-VEN-shun)
A convention is a meeting. Political parties hold conventions every four years to choose their presidential candidates.

debate team (deh-BAYT TEAM)
A debate team is a group of people who compete against other teams by discussing a topic with two points of view. One team argues for the topic, and the other argues against the topic. A team wins by proving its point.

evidence (EH-vuh-dentz)
Evidence is proof of something. A committee from Congress looked at evidence against President Nixon that proved he had committed a crime.

impeach (im-PEECH)
If a political leader is impeached, he or she is accused of doing something wrong. Barbara Jordan was a member of the committee that had to decide whether to impeach President Nixon.

minimum wage (MIN-ih-mum WAYJ)
Minimum wage is the least amount an employer can pay a worker by law. Texas did not have a minimum wage law until 1969.

multiple sclerosis (MUL-tuh-pul skleh-ROW-sus)
Multiple sclerosis is a serious disease that affects the brain. Barbara Jordan had multiple sclerosis.

outstanding (out-STAN-ding)
If a person is outstanding, he or she stands out as being important, talented, or successful. Barbara wanted to be the most outstanding student at her high school.

Glossary

pastor (PASS-tur)
A pastor is a leader at a church. Ben Jordan became a pastor at a Baptist church.

platform (PLAT-form)
In politics, a platform is the ideas and beliefs that a politician or political party supports. Members of the Democratic Party meet every four years to discuss the party's platform.

political party (puh-LIH-tih-kull PAR-tee)
A political party is a group of people who share similar ideas about how to run a government. The Democrats and the Republicans are the two biggest political parties in the United States.

politician (pawl-uh-TISH-un)
A politician is someone who works in government, such as a senator or the president. Barbara Jordan was a politician.

politics (PAWL-uh-tiks)
Politics refers to the actions and practices of the government. Barbara Jordan retired from politics in 1979.

practice (PRAK-tiss)
To practice law is to work as a lawyer. Barbara passed an exam in 1959 that allowed her to practice law in Texas.

preachers (PREE-churz)
Preachers are religious leaders who give sermons at churches. Reverend Howard Thurman was one of the most respected preachers in the country.

prejudice (PRE-juh-dis)
Prejudice is a negative feeling or opinion about someone without a good reason. African Americans have often faced prejudice from white people.

segregated (SEH-grih-gay-ted)
If something is segregated, it cannot be used equally by all people. Many places in the South were once segregated, so African Americans either could not enter or were separated from white people.

sermons (SUR-munz)
Sermons are speeches about religion, usually given at churches. Barbara remembered the sermons that Reverend Thurman gave.

sorority (suh-ROAR-eh-tee)
A sorority is a club for women, especially at a college. Barbara Jordan was a leader at her sorority.

term (TERM)
A term is the length of time an elected official holds an office before another election. A Texas senator's term is two years.

theology (thee-AWL-oh-gee)
Theology is the study of religion. Reverend Howard Thurman was a professor of theology.

Index

Further Information

Books

Blue, Rose. *Barbara Jordan* (Black Americans of Achievement). Chelsea House, 1992.

Gulotta, Charles. *Extraordinary Women in Politics.* Chicago: Children's Press, 1998.

Jones, Veda Boyd. *Government and Politics* (Female Firsts in Their Field). Broomall, PA: Chelsea House, 1999.

Web Sites

Visit the University of Texas Barbara Jordan Page where you can read Jordan's speeches at the impeachment of President Nixon and at the 1992 Democratic National Convention:
http://www.lib.utexas.edu/Libs/PAL/jordan/

Learn more about Barbara Jordan:
http://pcl-a153.lib.utexas.edu/txtell/stories/j0001-short.html
http://www.rice.edu/armadillo/Texas/Jordan.html
http://www.elf.net/bjordan/

Read about the Barbara Jordan Historical Essay Contest:
http://www.utexas.edu/world/barbarajordan/

Read interviews with other leaders who remember and honor Barbara Jordan:
http://www.pbs.org/newshour/bb/remember/jordan_1-17.html